ELEVEN MILES TO JUNE

ELEVEN

MILES TO

JUNE

poems

HA KIET CHAU

GREEN WRITERS PRESS *Brattleboro, Vermont*

Printed in the United States

10 9 8 7 6 5 4 3 2

Green Writers Press is a Vermont-based publisher whose mission is to spread a message of hope and renewal through the words and images we publish. Throughout, we will adhere to our commitment to preserving and protecting the natural resources of the earth. To that end, a percentage of our proceeds will be donated to environmental and social / racial justice activist groups. Green Writers Press gratefully acknowledges support from individual donors, friends, and readers to help support the environment and our publishing initiative.

Giving Voice to Writers & Artists Who Will Make the World a Better Place
Green Writers Press | Brattleboro, Vermont
www.greenwriterspress.com

ISBN: 978-1-9505841-4-7

COVER AND INTERIOR ART:
Watercolors by the poet.

Printed on recycled paper by Bookmobile.
Based in Minneapolis, Minnesota, Bookmobile began as a design and typesetting production house in 1982 and started offering print services in 1996. Bookmobile is run on 100% wind- and solar-powered clean energy.

For my little rainbows

ACKNOWLEDGMENTS

Grateful acknowledgment is made to the following publications where some of these poems first appeared:

"Pretty Skirts" *Off the Coast*
"50 Tallulahs in Santa Cruz" "Recluse on Lombard Street"
  Columbia College Literary Review
"The Hunger Artist" "Stillbirth" *Backbone Press*
"A Woman's Warfare" *Ploughshares*
"340 Kilometers of Madness" *Tule Review*
"A Streetcar Named Desire" "November 30, 1998" "Halfway
  Home" *Duende*
"Imagine Us Inside" "In Her Yellow Dress" *New Madrid:
  Journal of Contemporary Literature*
"Salt Lake Sisters" *Two Thirds North*
"Conformity in the Streets" *Dim Sum: Asia's Literary Journal*
"Beach Waters" "Lilac Wine" *Hawai'i Pacific Review*
"Killing Time" *Fjords Review*
"Glass Reflections" *Gravel: A Literary Journal*
"Murder a Tree" *Up the Staircase Quarterly*
"Before 30" "Ten Thousand Baby Stars" "Broken Aftermath"
  "The Brown Fedora" "Rage in Ripping Art" *Toad Suck
  Review*

"Lychee Tree and the Other Woman" "A Man Kissing
   A Woman Kissing Honey" *Asia Literary Review*
"Virginia Slims and Hawk Eyes" "Woman vs. Self "
   "Reverie" *The Lincoln Underground: An Independent Literary
   Magazine*
"Cocoon" *Reunion: The Dallas Review*
"Fitting Inside a Sphere" "White Lies" *Brickplight*
"Experimentation" *Ayris Magazine*
"Birdie Fly, Birdie Stay" *Lunch Ticket*
"100 Degrees Heat" "Maze Black Night" *The Riding Light
   Review*
"A Bird's-Eye View" *Everyday Other Things*
"1930" *Gold Man Review*
"Digital Romance" *Kalyani Magazine*
"What-If and Maybe" "American Dream" *Stoneboat Literary
   Journal*
"Blossoming Zhou Civilization" *Eunoia Review*
"A Starry Night on Fire" *Flutter Poetry Journal*
"A Mélange at 12:19" "Language Fluid As Milk" *The Literary
   Nest*
"Zigzag Outlines" *Stone Highway Review*
"Nocturnal Rain" *Rockhurst Review*
"The Sculptor's Mold" *Zaum*
"A Hummingbird Named Havoc" *The Meadow*
"Wingless Sommer" *Mission at Tenth Journal*
"Ex-Collision" *Dressing Room Poetry Journal*
"Lonely Wolf and the City" *Star 82 Review*
"At Home with Confucius" "Dakota" "Color of Tea in
   Autumn" *Clarion*

CONTENTS

Close-Up

Wide-Shot

Fade-Out

Close-Up

Pretty Skirts

A very hungry night, gurgling stomach,
lunging wolf mouth.
The city opens its gates, flashes a fang, a snarl.
Menacing shadows, white rain,
auto headlights pour like butter
down the avenue of my body.
Strangers and their Lolita obsessions.
They give me candy,
lure me into dirty alleys.
What would Mama say if I were to taste
forbidden sweet, wash it down
with scotch, a fistful of aspirin?
Police sirens, helicopters up top,
another manhunt, another woman down,
another night, unfazed.
Strangers run like felons through parking lots,
swift crooks, they never get busted.
In my neighborhood, crime and violence
occurs periodically like rainfall
and little girls don't get to wear
pretty skirts in the rain.
They grow up wearing masculinity—
walk like fathers, talk like brothers.
The role of a man, I rehearsed it well,
on cue, a method actor, tough and unafraid.
Strangers often mistake me as sir,
I don't answer to ma'am.
On the streets, I'm nobody's daughter,
nobody's woman.
Get them hands off me, I'm untouchable,
indestructible.

Ten Thousand Baby Stars

The moon is the protector, the mama in the sky.
The stars are her babies, all ten thousand of them.

On moonless nights, they twinkle and whimper,
pounding rain on Victorian rooftops
and concrete pavements.

It is seafood night. Sixty-two degrees out, nippy.
The raw stench of crabs and clams drifts out
to the backyard.

Ma is in the kitchen deveining shrimps.
She keeps an eye on us from the window.

We waltz for her like vaudeville dancers,
whirling in our ballerina hoopskirts.
Bodies pivoting, falling to the grass, woozy.

Ma disappears from view.
Rain douses our hair, drips down our necks.
Ma comes back into focus.

A flash of her jade bangle, her curly permed hair.
Her arm reaches for a plate in the cabinet.
She disappears again, longer this time.

We wait for her on this moonless night.
The baby stars and the universe lie still.
Trees whisper, a pinecone drops to the ground.

Ma reappears at the window.
She unties her apron, gestures for us to come in
from the rain.

The stars stop whimpering.
Monsoon clouds part like velvet drapes.
The moon emerges from the backdrop.

Mama was always there watching her babies.
She was never gone.

Broken Aftermath

Glass shattering, glass echoing
in the house, upstairs, downstairs, in my ears.
Fear trembled, I shook like a strip of grass
in wind—I just broke my father's antique
glass table.

Storming out of the kitchen, father's eyes
were dark rain clouds.
He pointed a long finger at me,
what did you do?
I stared guiltily at my ten-year-old feet.
Scared soundless—I couldn't tell him

I was playing make-believe, drinking hot
chrysanthemum tea in a dim sum cafe.
I couldn't tell him the china cup leaped out
of my hand and fell onto his precious
glass table.

I was a jackrabbit in a meadow, petrified.
Father was an eagle in the sky, infuriated.

I hid behind the calm wings of my mother.
She reasoned with him–he sighed,
grabbed a broom, began sweeping
the broken glass into a pile.

The storm wasn't over—thunder boomed,
lightning zigzagged.

Daddy, I won't play make-believe anymore.

Mother motioned for me to go to my room,
father continued sweeping the floor.
He did not utter a word to me that night.
The next day, the glass table was replaced.

It was then that I knew my relationship
with my father had changed.

AMERICAN DREAM

A rare sunset as the United States salutes those tens
of Chinese families through a square cut plane window.
A proud soldier's hand rights the free, here we come.
Is it truly free, Papa?

America, suddenly the uniting of states, where all our
imaginings do not materialize—
a broad stretch from the optimistic land
Mama paints in her dreams sitting on a China bus.
Her dream flushes down the toilet.

A rundown apartment, limited English, mockery at school,
a backbreaking meat cutting job, cold long nights.
Neighbors as foreign as their curly Afro dos, their blonde goldilocks,
an acceptance we crave, only to be aimed with stones.
Chase our yellow skin right back into Chinatown.

Hail a flight, count the five yellow stars on the China flag,
this American dream is dying under dictating eyes.
The poor rot like ripe potatoes hungrily eaten for dinner.
Nothing to eat, must not waste, Mama says
as the rich rise like fat green trees.

Ching-Chong, poor little bananas, fresh off the boat taunts,
piss the poorness out of a poverty-stricken man.
This melting pot eats at us
as greedy carnivores take a chunky bite of our flesh.
No need to steam and scorch our ancestors' black hair
and yellow complexion until we are white and pasty.

Our breaths shut up as we suffocate in a huge boiling pot
melting alongside sugar cane sticks.
We shrivel like weedy straws in a cage.
Tormentors suck out all of our sweet bowed
politeness in this simmering blister.

Stand our ground, where's our voice?
This era, nasty and broken, senseless insults swinging
left and right—punches a deep prejudice in all of us.
We stare at our impending futures through beaten eyes.

SALT LAKE SISTERS

We are wanderers of geology,
paddling a boat on a lake that tastes like salt.
Cohabiting with amphibians, this lake is not ours,
it's an extension of ourselves in water.

Peer into an eyepiece, our see-through
reflections, clear as binocular vision,
adjust the focal range, the focus is on us:

two sisters clutching a boxful of dreams,
and if we were to drown them in the basin,
we'd be lost orphans—

who are we without something tangible
to hold onto?

You and your ukulele, me and my journal.
We're losing grip of each other on a lake.

Drops of acoustic, lyrics and four strings,
your clef notes, my verbs and nouns,
listen to them
            ricochet like pebbles off water.

From identification cards, to birth certificates,
our baggage, our minds and bodies
twined in algae and seaweed.

The end result has nature lamenting and
mother—

she, who seldom cries in the summer
expresses condolences for her daughters
in the deluge of rain, in sighs of grays and gloom,
carried all the way into autumn.

Zigzag Outlines

Sobbing in front of the Buddha altar.
Bowed head shaking.
Fifth child, a self-proclaimed adolescent sin,
slams the door on her strict family.
Father bolts the locks on her Americanized culture.
The Marilyns, the Jimmy Deans, the Sid Viciouses.
Kneel before the Buddha statue, beg a million mercies.
A rebelliousness perishes her black Gothic clothes.
Satan's hands wipe her dark pout, seizing her red wits,
howling a zany shriek like a zebra attacked
against the protesting whines of the helicopter engine.

Father's black thunder fumes.
Summoning strict storms.
Mother cracks her red lightning whip.
Twelve tick-tocks on the cuckoo clock strike past curfew.
Chinese myth roars in full force,
electrocuting a disobeying Cinderella, her yellow-dyed hair,
smoky black as God's rage, in a fierce sky awaiting punishment.

Juvenile delinquent, step down harder on the pedal,
claw a way out of this rolling thunderous maze,
like a Chinese Natalie Wood,
stuck among the seventeen sticky cobweb clouds.
Wave a flag stained with stars,
is it the China or the American flag?
Fly her Chinese-American roots down a dead end cliff.
Flap her bold, blue, slick wings.
Camouflage her sapphire arms against the turquoise clouds.
Kick her parent's scolds away, near a tiny glimmer of rainbow.

Blink back tears as father's fist plunk-plunks against her head.
Stupid girl, wake up, why are you wasting your life away?

Her independence, her womanhood,
stomping with elephant's legs, echoing,
cracking her liberal earth.
Crash Amelia Earhart's freedom,
flop like a fiddly heart down under,
as a yielding engine whimpers.
Testing its final limits. Fuel groaning for oil.
Clouds flinging her face down on her bed.
Sobbing.
Zigzag rumblings outline her two halves.
Her Chinese and American self.
No way home.

Eleven Miles to June

A long march to June. I roam and roam
under glittering constellations,
in seek of all things yellow.
Somewhere in the Midwest, a buffalo
is shot dead and a farmhouse is on fire.
Oh no, tonight, walls of gloom cave in.
Scarlet plumes of smoke and blood,
flames stronger than torrential rain.
Everywhere elms and beeches topple,
charred leaves, rusted trunks.
Mothers and children huddle and pray,
as men dig their way out of rubble
and mayhem. Early burials on the first
of spring, the poet inside me aches
for all things gone. In woods,
covered in cinder and ash, I walk and walk,
dreaming of home, roads and roads away.
I outrun wolves but can't escape
the lost child. Her voice is a teardrop
reverberating from the bottom of lakes.
Tempted to dive in—it is always she,
the inner girl, who glides me away
from the edge, reminding me of tomorrow
and the eleven miles to yellow.
As I head down a crooked trail,
above a smoke-filled sky, the sun rises
to a new day, and somewhere
in the Midwest, a baby lamb is born.
Mothers and children wake as men
rebuild what was once lost.

In hours of clarity, the sea swells with hope.
Light glows from the horizon.
Moving onward, I envision all things
yellow: banana trees and lion cubs
in India, acres and acres of daffodils
in Spain. These beautiful locations
and untold stories. I must keep roaming
'til I see gold, touch June.

A Hummingbird Named Havoc

Autumn nostalgia, jasmine tea and wonton soup,
the slow, heavy aroma of time passing.

I once walked there, danced over
a steel bridge, young. On a Macau hilltop,

flocks of hummingbirds soar, teaching
me how to spread my arms.

You swooped in with birthmarks
and scratches on your wings.

Your presence, complex as your riddle:
what caused you to bleed so much?

For months, fiction and lies, ghazals and secrets
fell like feathers and snow.

Our time was transient, ecstatic one minute,
despondent the next. When you left, owls nested

in the sequoias. Reasons remained
unknown and your silence in winter,

sunken and vast, cut open places that stung,
triggered old wounds, taught me lesson

after lesson on self-worth. A deep gash,
lullabies couldn't fill night's holes.

That spring, valleys quaked, islands flooded.
I fell out of the saddest reverie—a ten-story spiral

and amnesia came sudden like a seismic jolt.
All traces of blue vanished from my eyes:

flecks of sky, cups of ocean, colorblind
days, forgotten.

FITTING INSIDE A SPHERE

An abrupt landing, I feel my feet
hit grass and on a moonlit airfield—

a silver plane touches down on tarmac.

First time in a foreign city, adapting
to a new culture, a new language—

my body readjusts, my brain reinvents.

Try to fit a triangle inside a sphere,
I'm out of place, out of my comfort zone.

In this small town, my three-dimensional
points poke out like the arms of a starfish.

Directionless—tell me where to go next.

I am human—dying to evolve—
who am I really in this skin?

Assimilation is a slow process like
squeezing into a pair of skinny jeans,

tight at first, but after a bit of sweat
and struggle, it fits and now

I have to walk in them.

Lonely Wolf and the City

My mother tells me when I am
older and wiser in my twenties,
the world won't feel so big.
If I lose a penny today, I will find a shinier one tomorrow.
I am heading out for a walk and she
stuffs a peach pit in my hand,
so I can hold the city, feel how small it is.

In downtown San Francisco,
it is teeth-chattering cold even in the summer.
I am strolling down Union Square,
thinking about the things I once had and lost:
A blue-eyed Barbie when I was five, some kid stole it.
A leather bound journal when I was twelve, my father trashed it.
A brown-eyed boy when I was seventeen, I called it off.
Memories of adolescence, I couldn't keep them safe—
times of naiveté, fog, and uncertainty,
times when I didn't realize I was actually happy.

At a dumpling house in Chinatown,
a child's laughter is bright as a lantern.
From the second story window,
the aerial view of the city is impressive
like Shanghai in the early 1920's.
Tea parlors and candy shops,
elderly couples and young individuals
walking in hurry, in leisure through the streets.
The people of the city,
where are they all going?

I tell my mother the city is a lonely wolf.
It is the cafés and museums, the culture and people
who keep the streets jovial and energized.
In the evening gray, the city is vacant.
I'm two blocks from home
and the ants on the concrete are the only ones
who can hear a rumble at twilight,
the thud of a peach pit dropping
from my hand onto wheatgrass and soil.
The city is free to bloom again.

DAKOTA

Dakota is homeless, resting next to a stack
of comics, a jar of potpourri.
I take her down from the shelf.
She stares at me, her morose eyes blue
like the Indian Ocean.
I remember Mama had that same look
when Papa left two years ago—she
hasn't smiled since.
Dakota's pigtails stick like beeswax.
I unbraid her hair, shampoo her curls in the sink.
She smells like oranges and soap.
I can't scrub the sadness off her face.
She sits motionless in daylight as I sew
the rips and holes in her Cinderella dress,
smooth out the wrinkles.
Mama's calling my name.
I place Dakota back on the shelf,
abandon her for the day.
In the greenhouse, I follow Mama around
like a poodle as she waters plants,
shoos me away.
On a patio bench, I sit and count
all the popsicle sticks I've collected
over the summer.
Two hundred ninety-eight.
Rolling up my sleeves, I recount a third,
a fourth time.
Three hundred and one.
Yawning, my mind wanders to the clouds,
so many odd shapes, another miscount.
Three hundred and two.
Mama hovers over me, arranging

gardenias in a clay pot.
What are you gonna do with all those sticks?
I think of Dakota alone on a shelf, homeless.
I look up at Mama, *I'll build a dollhouse.*

Experimentation

In a field of shrubs and blackberries,
an earthquake occurred as I dreamt
of water and science.
I woke to a farmer calling me baby.
I was an embryo of a seed,
branches sprouting, arms and sticks.
My brain waves and neuroses jittered
at the contact of sun and nature.
I blossomed on solar energy,
grew into my body, evolved into a tree.
Standing in precipitation,
tall and modelesque,
I dare not squirm or fidget
as the farmer, infatuated with nature,
jotted notes, tested hypotheses.
I developed self-confidence,
accepted my scarred twigs, leafless body.
And when a cold front set in,
the weather became so intolerable
that the interaction between a farmer
and a tree had to conclude.
The day arrived when he fell
to his hands and knees,
tore me out of the earth,
freed me by the roots of my hair,
left me standing butt-naked
in the jungles of society,
where freedom felt strangely alien.
I am homesick for the life I once knew,
but the past was a practice test,
an experimentation,

designed for my future survival
to not topple over, to stand tall again
as I settle in on a new location,
a home up in the canyons.

In Her Yellow Dress

On a porch chair in summer humidity,
Ma sits and nibbles on a grape jelly sandwich.
She can't see me, nor can she see the sun.
The neighborhood kids are celebrating.
Fireworks and laughter spit—earth booms.

Ma shudders in her yellow dress, and I
recall that story she told me long ago
in Vietnam when bombs dropped
and war fumes damaged her vision–
robbing her of rainbows and orange skies,
deserting her in black ponds.

Ma licks grape jelly off her knuckles.
Tidbits of breadcrumbs slide from her lap
onto hot asphalt—she is unaware.
Two bluebirds idle near her bare feet.
They peck blindly at the crumbs, fly
away in tandem.

Raucous cheers roar down the avenue.
Firecrackers detonate—*bang*.
Ma squeezes her eyes shut.
She doesn't shudder, her body is stoic
as a fig tree rooted to rock-hard soil.
Sunlight shimmers on her yellow dress,
jade pearls, silver hair.

She opens her eyes, lashes flutter
like silk wings.
Ma senses my presence, mutters how her

skin is warm as desert sand.
The bluebirds are now perched on top
of a telephone pole, singing peacefully
as we converse over a pitcher
of lemonade in summer heat.

MURDER A TREE

The inside of a coconut is whiter than snow.
The evening misses the moon the way a honeybee
misses pollen, the way I miss color.

Biting into a boysenberry, juice streaks
down my chin like black ink
and rain.

We're living inside a cartoon.
Last night, I dreamt we hiked up
Runyon Canyon with the Smurfs.

Your blue skin complemented my violet hair.
You chuckle, tossing me a pack
of Crayolas in a Ziploc.

I color stop signs—teal, exit routes—orange.
I draw cars weaving in and out of the 405,
turnpikes leading me out of mazes.

At the crossroad of reality and make-believe,
you whisper, *go green light.*
My jeep wrangler rams into a tall redwood.

Severed branches, battered hip,
broken crayons, kaput wheel.
I see asterisks and dots, the size of M&M's—

the world spins like a merry-go-round.
You yell, *visualize green, it won't hurt as much.*
Watermelon rinds, jade bangles, emerald gems—

you know me. Damn, you know too much.
Green alleviates pain
as morning mist evaporates.

Surreal—
a multicolored arch stretches above a bridge.
Lock me up in a 6 x 8 cell.

I just murdered a tree and the sky unveils
the prettiest rainbow.

Before 30

Separated by a glass window, cracked,
the sky and me.
Hickory branches jabbing cumulus clouds.
Raindrops weep, ashes and pennies fall.
All morning, seagulls and planes intersect,
jet-wings chopping delta skies
at ten o'clock, bleed rain at ten o'five.
Separated by a wooden door, splintered,
me and her.
She's taking a bath, skinny dipping
in the ocean's tub.
I give her space, I burn my toast.
All morning, I can't get that noise out
of my head, a plane hurtling into
the Atlantic—the impact of a splash,
bird suicide.
A throb in my ribs, waters glint
like rubies on fire—the color of her eyes
after grief.
She wanted sleep, she couldn't sleep.
The babies keep her up all night.
She's been having visions of dying
before 30.
Behind the door, silence echoes
like the inside of a conch shell.
Paranoid, I check on her—empty pill
bottles in the sink—she's asleep.
We are wreckage from a collision.
A tail and wing there, a wallet,
a feather, a shoe over there.

All morning, bodies float face down
in the ocean.
Raindrops weep, ashes and pennies fall.
The babies won't stop crying.

Virginia Slims and Hawk Eyes

A snowman is melting on the lawn,
headless and rail thin, dripping down
5th avenue like a rivulet.
The Murphy girls are jumping in puddles,
splashing water on each other.
They yelp. I shiver and turn
from the window as Ma hides knives
and pill bottles in the pantry, padlocks it.
A hammer is pounding on metal somewhere.
I swallow aspirin to rid a headache.

The evening slows. Chopin nocturnes play
on the phonograph.
Ma and I sit on wicker chairs like little women
from the 1800s, sewing torn garments.
These melodic hours. These destructive thoughts.
Ma monitors me with hawk eyes.
I jab a needle in and out of a camisole.
My fingers bleed.
Ma thinks needles are weapons.
I'm not allowed to sew anymore.

A silver thimble rolls onto the oriental rug,
stops at the window.
I peer outside—barking dogs
are a distraction, vacant roads are an escape.
The snowman has melted.
He leaves behind a damp wool scarf.
The Murphy girls fight over it, tugging

and ripping the fringes.
Wine-color yarn—strands of browns
and burgundies disintegrate in their hands.

The evening dims. Down the street
the Murphy girls disappear,
flip-flops slapping asphalt.
The night grows chilly, *brrr* . . .
Ma hovers by the oven—chain-smoking
Virginia Slims, stick after stick.
White ribbons of smoke twirl around us.
Her hawk eyes can't see me in the haze.
I shiver, pop another aspirin.

Mommy Wasn't Wearing Any Clothes

1 AM—unplug all the lamps in Brooklyn.
Pitch-black, Mrs. Lee jolts awake from
a nightmare.
On the sofa, she lies like a corpse, her gaze fixed
on the window overlooking Hudson Avenue.
Headlights illuminate pieces of garment
strewn across the grass lawn:
lace bras, satin undies, sheer lingerie.

2 AM—flick on all the lamps in Brooklyn.
Neon-yellow, Mr. Lee rubs the sleep out
of his eyes.
On the bed, he peers out the window.
His wife is picking clothes off the lawn,
dumping them into a garbage bag.
He waits for her to come back inside.
He dozes off—a car door slams, she is no longer
there when he wakes.

3 AM—Mr. Lee is sick of his reflection sneering
from the window—who is that lunatic with
receding hair and scruffy beard?
When did he get this haggard, this callous?
In the opposite room, his daughter wails,
Mommy. . . . Mommy—
Mr. Lee chugs malt whiskey from a bottle,
yanks down the shades, buries his face
in his hands.

4 AM—he remembers
every. detail. from. last. night:

His wife on her knees picking up broken glass,
scarring her manicured hands.
Four-year-old Lucy crying hysterically as he tossed
underwear out the window in rage.
Shit. His daughter saw too much—Daddy dragging
Mommy by the hair out the front door.
Mommy begging Daddy to let her back in.
Mommy wasn't wearing any clothes.

November 30, 1998

The river is numb.
Cold as hell—I can't feel my toes, can't feel
my pulse.

The night Pa gambled all his money away,
two bullets fired through our window shattering
the antique vase and the Buddha statue
on the mantelshelf.
Outside, a black SUV gunned down the street,
doing 80, tires scratching gravel.

My little brother screamed as Ma plucked
glass off his face with a tweezer.
I tried distracting him from the sting—
flapping like Big Bird, hopping like Kermit,
pointing at the TV screen—*look, Jimmy, look!*
Sesame Street was no help, Jimmy cried
so loud, bells rang in my ears.

Pa staggered in after ten, beer spilling
from his dented Budweiser can when two
large men barged through the door.
When Pa said he couldn't pay off the debt,
they shot him in the leg, bang once, bang twice.
Ma shook in her apron dress.
The men eyed her up and down, forcing her
at gunpoint to leave with them.

Jimmy cried, I couldn't move.

The river is numb in November.
Pa's limping across Mulholland Dam,
clutching my little brother's hand.
The scars on his tiny face—visible in the dark.
Pa's calling my name through a megaphone.
He sounds far away.

The river is dead in December.
Canaries and frogs drift facedown in the water.
I am swimming and drinking the river,
gulp after gulp until I'm so heavy, I sink.
Ma must've felt this way too when she jumped
into the Atlantic the night Pa gambled
all his money away.

Beach Waters

If I dip my toes into the Pacific
I'll bleed, but I am risking it,
diving into her artic waves,
a glitzy disguise of yellow
stones and blue glass.
The sharp rays of the sun's
nose cut bluntly,
aquatic waters churn.
Schizophrenic tides,
tumultuous tosses and turns,
rock me north and south.
The off-and-on destructive
tendencies of the ocean's mistress,
a sea sickness, bashing cold,
sinking lifeboats, paddles,
and starfishes down under.
Her complex waves, weary
from rough play, take pity,
steer my body back to shore.
I should've never set foot into
the ocean—breakable woman,
you turn beach waters crimson.

GLASS REFLECTIONS

Her glass appearance startles,
unrecognizable woman.
I want to shampoo her matted hair,
zip up her bellbottom trousers,
iron her tank blouse, but she's
not a touchy-feely kind of gal.

She copycats my facial expressions
like the Mona Lisa.
If I furrow my brow, she'll glower.
If I stick out my tongue, she'll howl.
If I smear mint balm on her mouth,
she'll rebel, lick it all off.
I should love her, but I don't.

Internal dialogue is cruel.
Voices echo cold: *I can't look at her.*
Voices in denial: *I don't recognize her.*
A mirror shatters to smithereens,
our glass reflections crack like ice.
I sweep up the mess with a broom.
I can't pick up my broken bits,
don't want a new scar.

Wide-Shot

Conformity in the Streets

My legs carry me among women and men, babies and children.
I wince at the glare of the frying sun.
My body shifts in unbalanced strides. No one sees me.
New York wind combs and straightens my messy hair
· to strings of fine black silk.
Clouds atop are a mass of frozen ocean;
a blue elastic stretching for hours.
Streetlights flash green, red, and orange.
Our destination lies among the cars, the cafés, the shops,
and the gossipers.
Ours legs persist in walking
simultaneously with the flash of that little white man.
Careful not to collide into strangers,
so many heads like redwood trees in front of us.
The toss of a woman's brown hair, tall as a supermodel.
My 5´2˝ figure petitely falls in step with her.
Straight ahead to the right, I see
his backwards John Deere baseball cap.
Distracted, my gaze refocuses to the left.
An old lady mumbles to herself.
Cars immobile in traffic, donut smell drifts into our noses.
Avoiding all contact we stride as if we are leashed.
Conformity puts us in a race to the finish line,
towards the exact destination to nowhere.
I choose to walk, feeling anonymous.
Nobody sees me.
Suddenly, a stranger, isolated from the crowd,
from the opposite direction, walks towards us.
Oblivious to the raise of arched eyebrows,

his brown eyes pause on my face for a second.
Chaotic city streets swim in a blur of traffic.
He vanishes.
My face, motionless in his memory, will soon be forgotten.
So we keep moving,
and every now and then, there comes a new stranger,
strutting in our direction.
I'm still anonymous.
I'll take that stranger's route the next time.

A Bird's-Eye View

This is the morning after.
A bird's eye view of wreckage.
Mother Nature is nearby composing herself,
calming down after casting off a series
of phenomenal mood swings.
Her anguish simmers down to a careful boil.
I locate her grace at sunrise.
A brutal weekend of wind growling at dogs,
rain screaming at a passive earth.
She is hoarse and I am deaf,
the reaction to a hurricane, a devastation.
She makes no apology
for leaving a town in catastrophic ruin.

This is the morning after.
Navigating across a pale blue sky.
Black wings and bravery outstretched.
I am not an aeroplane, but a vertebrate,
a black raven soaring above a city caked
in heaps of brown destruction.
Pile after pile, an odor of death and loss,
garbage and dirt accumulating sky high.
I can flock to a warmer location down south.
Perch discreetly on the arm of a magnolia branch.
Indulge on breadcrumbs, berries, and caviar,
but I lost my appetite.

This is the morning after.
A migration route concludes with a purpose.
I am a black shadow of hope suspended,

hovering in midair over a town,
rebuilding for a second time from nothing,
reconstructing from nada.
I want that man who lost his mobile home
to examine
the sky in all its blue overtones,
the outspread of my sore, feathered wings,
the miles I have flown to partake in a mission,
to hold a city together.
I manage a high-pitched whistle.
He looks up, aware of my song in flight,
breathing steadfast, continuing in motion.

Imagine Us Inside

Twenty-one and broke, distancing ourselves
from the chipped glass and graffiti of the city.

Engine running low—liquor stores open,
headlights wink, prostitutes pace.

Up highways and swerving boulevards,
I inhale wind; a gust tickles the throat

of the night, a foghorn blares.
We park by the pond; the charcoal evening

is weary—blue moon shrivels like a balloon,
fades somnolently behind a sycamore tree.

Let's make-believe we live in one of those pretty
houses looming over the hills.

Imagine us inside. We say grace at brunch,
read fables at bedtime.

Look at that house on the far end, the one
painted white with a mailbox and a tree

in the yard, a worn tire swinging from
its branch.

At the lighted windows, two figures stand.
He is in one room, she is in another—

frozen silhouettes

staring dazedly out into the world, searching
for an escape, an answer in the dark.

We waited—their paths never crossed that night.
The lights flicked off in the house.

A STREETCAR NAMED DESIRE

Blanche introduced me to her blow dealer
the night before Halloween on Park Boulevard.
His name was Cruz and he looked like a young
Brando so we made out in a hookah smoke
alleyway under the Big Dipper.

24 hours later, in Daddy's truck waiting
for the green light, I saw a cop chase Cruz down
Macarthur—a block from Wong's Laundromat.
My mouth zipped shut as Daddy drummed
his fingers on the steering wheel, grumbling
about all the underage delinquents and hookers
in West Oakland.

Cars honked as Cruz shouted expletives
at the cop handcuffing him to a fence.
When he saw me slouched in the passenger's seat
of Daddy's truck, I mouthed, *where's Blanche?*
He darted his eyes across the street
at the curvy redhead in a leather miniskirt
and stilettos wiggling towards the black
Ferrari idling by the curb.

Blanche stuck out her ass, batted her Bambi
lashes at the faceless driver like a professional
before pocketing the money,
before stepping inside the car.
I held my breath as cars vroomed,
desire racing like wheels on wind.

Cruz watching me watch Blanche
from the side-view mirror.
Green light flashing. Heart beat waning.
Desire killing me with his point-blank stare.
If only desire could follow me home,
sneak into my bed, rumple my sheets.
Daddy doesn't have to know.

THE BROWN FEDORA

A woman in a brown fedora enters the stage.
I bet she stole that hat from Bogart in *Casablanca*.
I expect her to deliver a profound monologue.
Her words will trample all four corners of the stage.
She'll change my views about this man's world.
We'll step outside this square—
this box of logic and reasoning.
Little do I know, she dictates nothing, not a word.
Her eyes scurry below the brim of a hat.
I can tell she's looking at us looking at her.

On a whim, she doubles over, laughs a hungry laugh,
a hungry man laugh, a starving wolverine laugh.
My pulse races for this wild, wild woman
in this wild, wild world.
A low murmur sails through the audience.
A man picks up his coat, shouts an obscenity.
She hurls her hat to the ground.
She doesn't give a damn if he exits.
He changes his mind, takes a seat again.
She bends down to pick up the discarded hat,
strokes it like a horse's old mane.
A blast of wind storms across the stage.
The brown fedora blows away.
I swear it was in her hands two seconds ago.

I guess pleasure from anything real,
even from a man's fedora is brief.
It's like money, after the last nickel is spent,
it ends up in someone else's pocket.
We are left to interpret the silence of brief gestures

on stage, on all walks of life, among men and women.
My interpretations are different from hers, from his.
I leave the theater, sprint down 44th and Broadway,
chase after the symbolism behind
the brown fedora that got away.
A man's hat on a woman's head in the twentieth century.
It's like that Dylan song.

A Woman's Warfare

Hanoi streets on their last demise do not shine like yellow bananas.
The color of brown-spotted ripe bananas for straight eleven eves,
coated with layers of night fumes.
Seven women on their bicycles steer by a smoggy sundown.
Threatening bombs like alarm clocks tick in my ears
as war fumes snatch the pretty red *ao dai* dresses
off these women's hips,
rape their static, numb corpses set for tomorrow's entombment.
Counting the eleven minutes like the one hundred and one
diminutive black sheep who will never sleep,
they foreshadow deaths between exhausted yawns.

This chest that belongs to me leaps higher
than the string of soldiers evading gunshots up and down,
firing along mucky war fields.
This vision that belongs to me is stolen
like communist dictators seizing our possessions,
imprisoning our men until we are penniless,
a black vacuum of nothingness.
Wives wail giving birth on polluted street corners.
A terribly violent penetration precedes,
rings like panic sirens north and south, up and down,
east and west, through the surrendering city of Haiphong.
Women risk their lives under plunging bombs,
bemoaning on bended knees for their dying lovers.
Screaming bare babies crash down with fractured skulls.

Death wakes her up in an early mourning.
Men's tongues hemorrhage red blood and spew yellow vomit,
permeating the demised streets.
A naked offspring bawls like a burnt black cat
crying for milk when milk is not visible.
This 1972 Vietnamization aftermath,

the bloodshot eyes, so soggy, so sightless.
Sidewalks of a murdered Hanoi, ruined mounds
of black mountains barring women from ever climbing to the top.
Death tugs my hand, heaves me closer to a light.
Death fights for the fast pulse on my wrist,
for the eight-month fetus in my belly.
Our bodies run for a nearby underground tunnel, our single escape.
We hide like timorous red crabs under protective shells,
as mature men beg for a mercy they rightfully deserve,
for a more lenient peace.

50 Tallulahs in Santa Cruz

You sing my name, *Tallulah*, sing
it like poetry on the eve of my birthday.
I sleepwalk onto the beach
in my night gown.
Your voice echoes from the depths
of the bay—high notes,
dangerously hypnotic,
deeply haunting.
Stars glow like light bulbs as I
shortcut across the sand,
bang into boulders, cut my foot
on seashells.
The beach hurts. I'm not alone.
Women with auburn wigs
and champagne lips walk
alongside me, drugged and dazed.
Some stick thin, some pear shaped,
some voluptuous—
50 Tallulahs in Santa Cruz,
42 prostitutes and 8 poets,
all sleepwalk blindly into the sea,
entranced by a masculine voice
that calls our names, entices our lost
souls with music and longing.
Tallulah, where are you?
Tallulah, can you hear me?
Tallulah, I want you so bad.
Closer and closer to the edge
of the Pacific, my legs
sink into icy waves.
Invade my body, manipulate

my thoughts, you recite verses.
Adjectives sopping wet,
line breaks leaving me perplexed,
leaving me wanting more.
In mint green waters, you sing
on repeat, *Tallulah, Tallulah*—
Women moan, splash, writhe.
I'm the first to drown.

340 Kilometers of Madness

There's madness to the mind when it tangles
like hair. Drag a comb through the kinks.
Pain is deep-rooted. Give me a dose of anesthetics,
a shot of Canadian gin. Give me scissors
and Frieda mousse. I'll detangle frizz,
straighten and snip each loop and strand.
There's madness to the heart when it anticipates
the sound of a ringing phone. We hear nothing.
There's motive to silence—the wait breaks
us down like an old 90's jukebox.
You miss the grunge and Cobain,
the guitar banging, wild, coke-filled nights.
There's madness to the soul when we lose
composure. I've seen patience in two-hundred
year-old trees and caged parakeets.
You are not spruce nor am I bird.
Can you stand still, can I wait another hour?
There's madness, 340 kilometers of madness
from me to you.
You're a train wreck, I'm a hot mess.
We are velocity. We accelerate. We crash. We die.
In the next lifetime, let's return as trees.
I'll be a buxom willow, you'll be a sturdy
eucalyptus. We'll stand side by side
in the woods and fall in love with the cuckoos.
We'll learn patience then.

1930

I departed Earth last night, fell into a deep
slumber. Spiraling into the unknown, images
and numbers flashed like camera lights:
cocoa skin, emerald eyes, orchid petals,
and 24 street signs.
Here I was, traveling like a nomad, in and out
of two worlds, teetering on the cusp
of reality and fantasy. In an alternate dimension,
gravity pulled me backwards to 1930.
Life, once a shade of gray, unfolded
like a Technicolor film.
The streets of Shanghai were humid and smoky,
lined with bakery shops, opium dens,
dance halls, and secret brothels.
Whiffs of herbal incense and sesame buns
hung in the breeze. Percussion beats
pounded from an opera house.
Beep-beeping up and down the roads,
foreign cars and wooden rickshaws hurried past
strangers with exotic angular features
and brown cocoa skin—women in silk *cheongsams*,
men in pinstripe suits, *have we met before?*
On 24 Changzhi Road, near a street vendor,
I spun three-sixty, bumping into a boy
with eyes that glinted emerald—
a rich hue of jade and sea.
He placed a lavender orchid in my hair,
traced 缘分 on my palm, and murmured, *zaijian.*
Lifetimes must've passed like rivers between us.
When he fled down a back alley, petals wilted,

and I knew in dreams, nothing good lasted.
As temperature rose and the streets grew hot,
I hopped on a trolleybus—gravity pulling me out
of the city. That morning, after a deep
slumber, I returned to Earth.
Gazing out the window, face-to-face with reality,
another gray, overcast day—no hummingbirds
singing, no song to ease my morning blues.
Eyes closed, I could feel the faces, colors,
and liveliness of 1930 fading like a memory.
Oh, to be lost in dream state again.

A Starry Night on Fire

Bathing in a pool of hot lava.
A slow week of sun pouring sweat.
Indian summer sizzling by the bay.
Clams roasting on bonfire and to the left,
the reddest, sexiest bridge I've ever seen.
The sun is king on its throne, towering over my senses.
Morning and noon, he's the greatest cliché,
the fire to my black and white night.

A moon slinks in, foxy and sly.
A queen forces her way in at restricted hours.
I bathe here nude against yellow city lights.
As soon as the sun waves bye-bye birdie,
I let him watch me slowly put on a kimono.
We are neighbors to the sun and moon,
synchronized on a flat civilized sky.
A first in a decade, a yin and a yang,
the urgency of passion giving into heat.
We are in a Van Gogh masterpiece drinking stars.

Nobody sees us playing house.
Swanky kitchens, white picket fences.
A strange dynamic we live in, round and round.
The confliction of sun and moon under one roof
burning in circles.
His mood leans on my shoulder for a nanosec.
We fold origami fans to cool our auras.
A starry night on fire, his words harder to read
than a Shakespearean sonnet reduced to ash, to powder.
He points out a sexual tension,

detailed in explicit heat.
He points a finger at beautiful chemistry.
We have no time to analyze the meaning.
It's lying naked between us.

A Mélange at 12:19

Nirvana is closed. We detour past the teahouse
on the corner of Herb and Westwood, racing
like indigo children up the Janss Steps.
A magical, razzle-dazzle night on top of the city.
If we count backwards from z to a, it's possible
to levitate and touch Neptune's 14 moons.
Electricity, we feel it all night, we feel it
blazing inside a kerosene lamp, in murmurs
and sighs, in air kisses, and au revoirs.
Rub your palms against the magenta sky,
it won't hurt. Cool off as conversation
blooms like French roses, skittle-sweet.
Ask me to be your empress.
I'll wear your Napoleon crown.
The night paces like a movie, we improvise
like Bogart and Bacall.
Unscripted banter. Natural chemistry.
They call this movie magic—a mélange
of rhyme and ultraviolets.
Sum up the night in two syllables: profound.
Flip a sandglass upside down. Rewind.
I want six more minutes to marvel
at fireflies glowing in the dark, wings slick
as oil and lava.
Let's not look for a happy ending.
There's more to our story. Fast forward.
If we walk past a café named *Intermezzo*
at 12:19, mandolins will play
the perfect melody.
We're not touching, but I think I've touched

you before sometime in the 17th century
on a gondola in Paris.
We take the long route home.
Music tinkles. Zephyr and dandelions drift.

Six a.m. Sunrise

My sweetness for a seasoned
tangerine sunup rises superior
before your six a.m. morning eyes.
Sitting cross-legged on a quixotic
Aphrodite mountain peak,
we watch the spark of orange
snuggle cheek-to-cheek
with the indigo dimples
of crane-shaped clouds.
The coating of illumination splashes
over the blueness of the wincing skies
and a ray of pumpkin luster
entices your eyes.
Shades of sunny splendor wriggle
their way into your sunlit gaze
and I fall in love at six a.m. sunrise.

Language Fluid as Milk

Conversing about Cham art in a café uptown, we tremble.
Glare of candlelight, the moon at twilight, your lips tremble.

Glass clinking, words and jazz mingling, latte brewing.
Me and you sip hot mocha, your lips tremble.

We talk spirituality until daybreak, I'm consciously
awake, teach me purpose, your lips tremble.

Language fluid as milk, translate the word *dazzling*
into Vietnamese for me, your lips tremble.

Loosen your polka dot tie, undo the knot, tell me the name
of the monk praying on a mountaintop, your lips tremble.

Tap your cigarette in my ashtray, blow smoke, tell me
in detail *The Tale of Kieu*, your lips tremble.

Emotion in your voice moves up and down like sun rising
at 6 A.M., sun dropping at 6 P.M., your lips tremble.

Mocha aftertaste on my tongue, mumble *tam biet*
at the last hour of conversation, your lips tremble.

Three winters zip by like bicycles in Saigon.
Eyes shut, I see rice fields, I see brown rivers, I see your lips tremble.

Romancing a reflection on a café window, lean closer,
say *Darling, I'm not a figment*, your lips tremble.

NOCTURNAL RAIN

A sleepless city shrouded
in a continuum of gray.
Downpour of late night showers,
up and down, a teeter-totter storm,
a light and heavy fluctuation.
Lights out, power off,
the rain fluid as a menstrual flow,
a black cherry drip.

Dancing rain, an erotic tempo.
Pointy branches tap
like fingers on windowpanes.
Folger's coffee and insomnia,
restless hours before dawn stirs.
Baby, undress the night
the way you would peel
the skin off a citrus fruit.
Your index finger is a hook
reeling me in, pulling me out
of shadows and dark woods.
Tell me again the tale
of the panther and the lamb.
Up close, words sound personal,
anticipation growls at the climax
of desire and danger.

Rhythms of rain and pulse
shake like maracas.
Wind rages onward, exhales.
A cigarette in your mouth,

you blow perfect O's.
We are ash after the fire dies low.
Rain drips softer now.
We curl into fetal positions,
drowsily succumb to sleep
until electricity returns.

STILLBIRTH

An embryo's heartbeat paces
fast like the crescendo of a song,
an upbeat tempo.
In the deep of the night
a crescent moon is bent like an ear,
as the heart quiets and listens.

Low murmurs in the secret dark.
You rest your head on my belly
and we spend minutes
whispering about our future,
about the name of our unborn child,
if he'll have your nose and teeth
or my black hair.

A hiccup in summer gust,
a pause in lilac breeze,
a fetus' heartbeat slows,
hangs on, and then
stops—
and that song
we've been listening to
for the last eight months
dies.
July's heartbreak,
a stillborn's final breath.

Silence on repeat at noon,
silence on rotation at night.
The silence, turn it off,

play something tranquil for me,
baby, please.
The sound
of a xylophone
is okay.
Melody muffles grief.
We can't hear each other in the dark,
it's easier this way.

And you're crying like a man
who lost his son.

And I'm crying like a woman
who lost her firstborn.

The Hunger Artist

Hollow as a baby pumpkin,
a hole forms in my stomach
after you're done scooping out
the seeds, slime, and pulp.
I once weighed fullness
on a supermarket scale, it was plump
as a melon, tipping the scale
at six pounds, 2 oz, but that weight
was aborted a week later
and emptiness felt like a glass
of tap water, half full.
In times of welfare and poverty,
you're carving a grin
on the outer shell of a pumpkin.
To be honest, it looks like
an upside down frown.
Seven o'clock before dinner,
I am reading about Kafka's
hunger artist fasting behind bars,
shedding skin and bones,
and when he lost consciousness
in a cage stuffed with skeletal
straws and public scrutiny,
I wonder if he remembered how
it felt to be full again?
You bring me a bowl of rice
to fill my belly, but what about
feeding my growling heart?
I've tasted the sweet and the salty,
chewed the solids and drank

the liquids, but nothing edible,
not even two bowls of rice
can lift the unbearable weight
of emptiness from the heart.

A Man Kissing A Woman Kissing Honey

Mama, how does it feel to love a man while living inside a moon?
I cried against a lemon tree whose leaves whistled like father did
nibbling a yellow egg yolk inside a mooncake,
lost in thought about the heart of a lonesome moon goddess.
Papa, a woodcutter destined never to chop down his cassia tree,
a rabbit's medicine unable to heal the fever of my night-time loneliness.
Mama, did you know I have never loved a man before?
I feel him every mid-autumn when he cries over a caged butterfly
whose legs moved like mother did when father kissed her upside down.
Breaking this myth with the woodcutter's axe in his hand,
I watch through a moon's crater how he fingers the rosebuds of her
     wings.
She becomes a butterfly suffering through the moon's metamorphoses.
A moon goddess does not know how it feels to love a man.
I can taste him on my tongue as I bite into his golden lemon hanging
on an eternal tree impossible for an enchanted axe to chop down.
His voice echoes past mythic meteoroids and colliding comets in space,
hollering that kissing me is a man kissing a woman kissing honey
from a butterfly's deathless lips.
Inhaling the perfume of his caged butterfly fluttering free
to the lunar surface of the harvest moon, a lantern tucked between
     her legs,
he pledges to Cassiopeia the rescue of a lonely woman, a rabbit,
and a woodcutter trapped tragically inside a full moon.
Mama, did you know I want to fall in love with a man?
He collapses ladder after ladder climbing the night, but can't save me.
I'm a broken butterfly not liberated to love.
By morning, vanishing behind the gloom of the sun, the moon does
     not exist.
I belong inside a myth. He belongs inside a reality.
Mama, I know how it feels to love a man while living inside a moon.

Hanoi, Circa 1842

You were sea deep. Crystal blue. Wise and worldly.
I was black lace, adrift in waves, dizzy and disoriented.

On days when monsoon clouds wept, your tides held
the antidote. I swam alongside angelfishes, crossing

shorelines. I flew with condors, circling mountains past
the meridian, on the hunt for a cure. Planets realigned.

Destiny blew incense in our faces. We met
beneath the temple bridge by the canal. The sky

swelled, distorting the temperature of sunset, peach fuzz
to hot pink. This was Hanoi at its finest, circa 1842.

When we collided, the ocean's heart rate shot up.
Synchronicity was at work, volcanoes gushed, magma erupted.

We were poet and traveler, hero and heroine, surviving
the carnage of war. We bled, we knew how to stifle hurt,

how to channel grace after defeat. Bridges separated us,
streams led us on opposite routes, continents apart.

I swam for days in the Hongze Lake, you sang hymns
to console grieving clouds. Our beginning was a whirlwind.

Midpoint had us kneeling—the earth snapped in half, divided
at the equator. We held on, agreed it was not the end.

Our storyline was archaic, buried centuries deep
in age-old paintings, in silk handscrolls and tea leaves,

retold countless times—details frayed and altered over
the years, so abstract and delusive, we became mythic.

MAZE-BLACK NIGHT

107 degrees Fahrenheit, leaves fry
like gold chips on the sidewalk;
potato crispy.
In the afterlife after sex, I perspire—
hot sweat.
Morning and night swap colors,
six a.m. orange, ten p.m. gray.
Temperature rises, an ice cube
dissolves on my tongue.
Slipping off my underwear, I imagine
swimming nude in Lake Erie.
Maze-black night, a light bulb flickers
in the dark caverns of my mind.
The ceiling fan rotates on high.
Freight trains rumble—closer and
closer, headlights beam.
In front of a speeding train, I can't
move—my legs stuck
like telephone poles to concrete.
Cargo spilling onto the tracks,
steel rails against my fractured
hip—I wake,
dripping hot sweat.
A car stereo plays reggae outside.
Gasoline and hookah smoke seeps
through my screen window.
A motorbike guns down the street.
Some girl cusses, a boy laughs,
Corona bottles clink.
This fast-paced world whirls

in a circle—I'm lightheaded
from square-dancing, dream-sleeping.
My back against the wall—alone
on a Wednesday, freight trains
rumble nonstop.
I can't find a door out of this
maze-black night.

Lilac Wine

Outside my window, the moon
is a limestone marble, it looms full,
bigger than a silver quarter.
I want to hold it like I own it, but
it is beyond reach, it belongs in the sky,
not in my palms.
The moonlight exposes shadows,
long and short on the sidewalk,
stick figures of men in grey ties,
stumbling in the drunk night,
smelling of guilt and lilac wine,
taking the usual route home.

Down the street, a chanteuse sings
a cappella from a blues bar.
Her tone is a lullaby drifting
into my half-open window.
At a quarter past midnight,
water runs in the kitchen,
a tea kettle whistles, disrupting
the flow of movement in my dreams.
When did you get home?
You turn off the burner, put out
the fire that once ignited us, excited us.
Careful now, the kettle is hot.
You rinse pain under cold water.
The sting hurts like hell, doesn't it?

In my bedroom, a brass doorknob
turns a centimeter, then a wide inch.
You come in, cross the threshold

like an illusive shadow, slipping
under my linen sheets.
The chanteuse ends her song
in a low hum, her voice breaking
with sadness as you curl up against me,
fall asleep like a baby.
For a naive minute, I make-believe
you belong here, that you are not
a shadow playing tricks, slipping in and out,
coming and going as you please.
I pretend you smell clean like soap,
not cheap lilac wine.

Lychee Tree and the Other Woman

Sorry to the second concubine craving the fruit
on a pregnant Guangzhou lychee tree.
First wife crying, her runny eyes, her creased unlucky palm lines,
picking lychees for the younger woman.
Brown old leaf not chlorophyll green in her youth,
breathing naively, hanging like suicide
on his jagged branch, nervous of neglect,
a woman's old age dipping to the ground, useless
to the emperor tree.

How invasive flirty honeybees are, poking their busybody
mouths into the emperor's rotten lychees, old, yet still tempting.
Jealous mottled moth flutters, trembles her parting wings.
To be one of the leaves on the emperor's lychee tree
and not to be a woman.
What's the difference?
Suffering for his attention, she is the leaf shrinking
to the ground, drying his ancient memory,
as a new tantalizing leaf materializes.

Sorry to the second concubine, for a third concubine
will take your place.
A green chrysalis opening up, upstaging the leaves.
All leaves anticipate the other lovely woman,
wait for this banded peacock butterfly to emerge
with giant green wingspans, seducing your emperor,
flaunting her six needle legs in his tree, summoning old leaves
to shake lychees into a basket for her.
Four wings doubling to eight monarch wings.
Interlacing. Quaking his twigs.

Seducing his brown bark as his sap drips
leisurely to the yellow grass.
Leaves cannot speak, but still the first leaf senses,
says nothing about the other woman, and the others
that will follow.

BLOSSOMING ZHOU CIVILIZATION

A feminine Adam, a masculine Eve ponder their reality
in a thief's cringing love poem.
Sore shoulders unwind against the timbered flesh of a plum blossom
    tree.
Sitting side by side, this man, this woman, on this Jing-Zhe,
this wakening of insects, has bell crickets chirp-chirping in a moody
    frenzy.
Pink-white petals sprinkle confetti, dangle onto pokey string lashes,
as Eve's slanted eyes pinch shut in a cozy line.
A poetic thief bargains for their bodies from a generous God,
an enticing apple lures them,
a magnetic pull inside the Zhou dynasty, an emergence,
the blossoming of Chinese civilization.

A poet's stolen daydream,
cunning upon my back on an antique temple bench.
Eyes a thin line, follow the monks' mouths moving,
revisit my 770 BC era. A lost mellow, woozy flash.
Aha! Adam, my charming emperor, my father.
Eve, my divine empress, my mother.
Stain brown skin. Glowing. Colored black hair. Stunning.
Modeling a manly pig tail, Eve chuckles.
Simple spring noon, grueling hours, lumber axing,
handpicking red satsumas from syrupy branches.
Coy rabbits, wily serpents gaze wide-eyed at two nude presences.
Hanfu seamstresses, wrap Adam's body in a *shenyi* robe.
Cuddle Eve's curves with a flowery *qipao*.
The awakening of Chinese civilization.

Winged arms looping around propped knees,
a sad Adam, a sick flicker, a misty moment for a thief's roaming eyes.
Daydreaming heads lean against the woody plum tree bark,

a yearned melodramatic reminiscence
for the thirty days left before April's departure.
A classic love cliché, the throwing up of cringing dragonflies.
Surprise ending for a thief's love poem.
Eve daringly smooches Adam on the lips,
creating the big bang of Chinese civilization.

THE SCULPTOR'S MOLD

A sculptor's hygienic hands mold
my unclothed limbs, dusk to dawn.
Smooth her two crafty fingers upon my fruitless spine,
pinch my hip's lower flesh.
Her stripe of morning glow scratches my knees,
measures my inflexible waist.
She times a sunflower's pollen blowing north
towards my tremulous bottom lip, down my uneven chin,
watering my eyes.
An affective artiste longs to paint my skin olive,
tattoo Chinese calligraphy upon my arm,
shove my frown to a still smile.
Her bare lungs die to swallow succulent morsels
from my poisonous throat.
Her rainbow hues mix clay, stir blotches, the cascade
of dye—oranges, yellows, innovative slabs of red.
She dips her fingers into a smudging puddle, dabbing
my decayed mouth an edgy, nervous shade,
redder than the curly peel of a naked apple
fondled by her paintbrush on this dreary afternoon.
Eavesdropping paint cans cling-clang
against her patterned marble.
Biting my lower lip, her lion canine bores
upon my plump virginal mouth,
flaring raw as an apple's flesh before
the caramel clogs my clay throat.
Scampering scarlet, choking under the stroke
of her paint-splattered hands.
Her nomadic taps, pats, travel upon my teeny ears.
A fifty-foot woman, squeezing my little nose,

sharpening my twenty-two pieces of cracked,
chalky reactions to her liking.
Her index, middle fingers travel along my toes
to the chopping of my hair, perfecting my Mona Lisa
smile with her walking hands.
My luminosity waning, her breath upon
my ceramic neck, wrestling the aroma
of her paint oils, becoming her porcelain statuette.
My skin a tinge of stoic olive, my inert frown,
now an imitation of my sculptor's smile.

Rage in Ripping Art

Sundays etched on my mind like paintings
from the impressionist period.

Mornings spent exploring the fine arts,
drawing figures, abstracts, and landscapes.

The streets smell rich—a mix of Starbucks coffee,
charcoal sticks, and newspaper ink.

Dawn peeps in through the blinds, reflects
squircles of light across the dresser mirror.

I see you hunched over a canvas,
fingernails dirty from watercolors and acrylics.

There's soap in the sink, but you're not
ready to wash your hands.

Colors can rile emotions, disturb moods.
There's frustration in the process of creating.

There's rage in ripping art with bare hands,
mutilating what was once creatively whole.

Those townscape paintings, sunkist skylines,
backyards and neighborhoods—lonely

sceneries without people, why did you tear
all of them into halves?

Should've stopped you, should've told you,
your paintings breathed life.

I was a river next to that fisherman's bridge,
you were a tree next to that gingerbread house.

We could've lived till we're a hundred
in all that color, all that detail.

Fade-Out

Recluse on Lombard Street

The day stretches long, yawns like a lazy
basset hound. I peek out of the wood blinds.
The Ziegfeld sisters sing and play
patty-cake in their yard, sucking on
peppermint sticks.

The older girl loses a rose knit scarf
in the wind. The younger girl drops candy
in the snow. They don't notice me behind
the stained glass window. My porcelain
reflection hasn't seen sunshine in months.

On Lombard Street, snowflakes descend
on bark roofs and chimney pots, blanket
the town in soft mounds of white.
The Ziegfeld sisters skip back inside their
little brick house.

I move from the window to the rocking chair,
spend the afternoon penning letters, ink
stains my nails blue. In the evening,
the phone rings and rings. A mantel clock
chimes. The hours darken and slow.

I button my fleece coat, walk down the hall
to the cedar door. Hands shaking, I unbolt
the locks, turn the knob, step out into the chill.
On this snowlit evening, miles of empty roads
lie untraveled—and tangled on an oak branch

is a torn rose scarf, fringes motioning
like fingers in wind, come out, come out.
In the distance, a crow releases a piercing caw,
flies north. I shiver and make a left down
Lombard.

KILLING TIME

In order to eliminate questions
weighing heavy as a sack of rocks
on the scale of human consciousness,
you kill time.
Bury your head in arithmetic.
Busy a fraction of your day calculating data
to get to the sum of all equations.

You drown out emotions that hassle.
Keep variables and formulas
at close proximity.
Drink nothing, consume nothing, but math.
Awful for the abacus in a corner cabinet,
sneezing dust, hoarding grime,
it has not been utilized in months.

Mission accomplished at a fifty-fifty ratio.
Time travels further than predicted.
Life, nonetheless, festers at a standstill.
The day is young and hair turns gray.
Loads of life questions,
very few definitive answers.
Newton's law of motion is not at fault.
I dare to disturb the solace
of a mathematician at work.

Incredible, isn't it, the power of physics.
The satisfaction to a proven theorem.
The measure of quantity and space,
traveling from a to b in a matter of minutes.

Adding x, subtracting y for a conclusion.
I wish it were that basic, that easy,
to apply the same scientific formula
to all the issues stacking heavy as textbooks
on the human mind.

Mass equations, when solved correctly,
will always contain the right answer.
But you're a mess at 3 A.M.
trying hard to figure out a solution
to alleviate the troubles weighing down
on the human soul.
You know it's not that basic, not that easy
to resolve all of life's issues,
not in the course of one day.

WHITE LIES

Baking in the white of winter,
flour and powder, vanilla splotches on
our aprons, a snowfall in the kitchen.
Our cake on the countertop
represents life in layers.
A first layer of bread on top,
a coat of cream in the middle,
a second layer of bread on the bottom.
Our triumphs and failures
stacked on top of each other.
We fight for a seat on the top tier,
nose-dive two stories down,
skin our knees, bruise our chins.
We are squished, veins and joints
on the verge of snapping
in a claustrophobic town,
sandwiched between a sky on top,
an ocean on the bottom.
Some rainbow sprinkles,
an eruption of color might jazz up
our moods, stifle our discomfort.
We decorate our cake with frosting,
feed each other lies over cups
of cold milk and sugar cubes,
tell ourselves life is oh so sweet.
Our objective is to keep from
dropping in water, from drowning.

100 Degrees Heat

Wives weep alone in bed
as bamboo grass sways side to side
like a dancer's hip.
Blow an eyelash, blow these women's
troubles down a wishing well.
Fan blows cold gusts,
sun squints hot tears.
A ballerina sniffles, dries her eyes
with a handkerchief.
Twirling on her tippy toes, she
seduces a silver fox snoring
under the shade of a walnut tree,
come here.
Power off, fan stops spinning,
wives stop weeping,
ballerina stops pivoting.
In 100 degrees heat—drink winter.
Swallow ice chips, think of alpine
glaciers and snow cones.
Imagine fucking the wind until it
groans, until foxes purr,
and berry shrubs tremble.
Power back on, electricity restored.
Fan blades whirl, a bicycle wheel
rolls down a hill.
Chaotic wind muffles all noises.
A ballerina pulls off her tutu,
lies motionless on the grass.
I wonder if she's still breathing.

Wingless Sommer

If she was a seagull she would've
changed her mind,
escaped death before hitting
water, ripples of salt.
Halfway down, she'd flap her
impaired wings,
muster strength to survive,
fly skyward, shoot right back
up like a NASA rocket into
the cotton blue, but

Sommer didn't get to change her mind.

Troubled and high on suicide bridge,
she pictured herself as a bird
when she flew off the lower deck,
a facedown plunge, 240 feet
into teal waters.
A chilling splash resounded
across the shivery bay
and life was over instantly.

Sommer didn't have wings to save herself.

Seagulls were the only eyewitnesses,
swooping down to the stony coastline,
squawking loudly,
commotion-crazy.

BIRDIE FLY, BIRDIE STAY

When voices hush, the night lies down,
tucks itself under a bulky plaid quilt.

You're wrapped in sleep, snoring lightly,
as Coco saunters in from the rain, meows,

disappears behind an armchair.
I get up from bed, move hastily about the room

like a thief, stuffing a sweater, a scarf,
two nectarines into a rucksack.

5:56 A.M., a cab beeps impatiently outside.

My hand on the doorknob, my legs straddling
the doorway, I pause to hear you sleep-talk:

birdie fly, birdie stay . . . birdie, don't leave . . .

There are reasons to why we all come and go.

I'm not the best version of myself.

The commotion in my head loses epic battles.

The broken in my body needs repair.

I've been searching for nutrient and light—
a nest to escape from the November rain.

Sorry for shutting the door, for leaving the key
under the welcome mat, for not saying goodbye,

for coming and going like those women who
talk of Michelangelo.

Color of Tea in Autumn

She broke two pencils writing me a five-page letter.
I read three-fourths and slept through the last paragraph,

woke to find a window half-open, a pigeon on the sill.
The morning is a hollow cave. The bird's gone, she's gone,

leaving behind an eyelash. In bed, I am cloud watching,
wild geese flying, wings aligned, feathers white as rice.

The sky needs a tissue. It is drizzling uncontrollably. Will
the birds return this fall? I remember she once said:

to detach is to let go, so shut the attic window, pull down
the Roman shades, let me sit in black for thirty minutes.

Let the mood wash off in this mellow hour, let me forget
the color of dawn in her eyes, the color of tea in autumn.

In migration season, I guess no one stays in one place long.
Not college girls or gray pigeons with lives just beginning.

EX-COLLISION

Church bells chime in a quaint chapel downtown
the second your eyes land on my face.
I hear it distinctly in a Santa Monica grocery store,
twelfth of June.

I push my legs out of a mama cocoon.
You walk towards me, consciously slow,
like we're in a sci-fi movie.

Motion dawdles and that cubic foot of space
separating us—collides like a meteorite on earth.
If we stick out our arms, our clothes will touch,
our fingers, skin will meet static and spark.

Here we are, in the heart of a grocery store,
like strangers from another universe.
I'm scarcely breathing; you're silent as a mime,
windless and parched.

Say something, anything and when a little boy
in the cereal aisle calls you Daddy--
I hear church bells again, chiming louder than before.

Collisions in life, this one hits the hardest,
            bull's-eye.

I wish we were like two military jets in the sky,
one traveling west, the other heading east.
We'll swerve to the right, veer to the left,
avoid crash, trauma.

Canola oil, almond biscuits, and your son's smile,

that's what I'll remember after we're done
exchanging pleasantries, wishing each other well.

The exit door slides wide open.

I'm carrying a loaf of bread, a jar of peanut butter,
and a carton of milk to the car—
this collision with you will take a while
to digest.

Manhattan Refuge

We resist the urge to ooh and ahh as diamonds
dot every inch of the Manhattan skyline,
their five points flashing like disco lights.
Tonight, we discard our sneakers, cigarette butts,
and cheap beer cans on the sidewalk.
On impulse, we climb staircases barefoot,
halting at the ledge of the sky to catch our breaths.
Fifty stories up, we could've been mighty eagles
or fighter jets—
if we're not careful, we could've fallen
to the bottom of traffic.
The future's a thrill ride.
Unknown twists, cartwheel turns.
Hair-flying-in-our-faces.
Let's make a pact, let's solemnly swear
to journey up, not down.
Let's forget the noise from below, sirens blaring,
canines barking, horns beeping.
Let's spit fire and release anger,
break free from cycles of self-destruction.
Let's de-stress, breathe in and out—remind
ourselves we're still alive.
On top of the city, dreams are possible,
no one's around to tell us we can't.
In our private refuge, away from the chatter,
the gossip, and the hustle of the city,
we're just two young rebels,
drunk-howling at the moon, belting aloud
our frustrations and fears.
No one's around to stop us from unleashing
our pent-up emotions on this mischievous night.
We're safe here.
We don't have to run anymore.

Dear Andrew

A bouquet of calla lilies in my hands.
I curtsy a bow, I blow a departing kiss.
I rush off center stage to neon exit arrows.
This time around, there is no audience,
no swift getaway.
In a crowded apartment on Strathmore Drive,
I return the lilies, deceased and smushed.
We can't fit a kiss inside this room of clutter.
I fumble for an excuse to leave.
A screen door claps shut behind me.
A mad storm unfurls, tugs four corners
of my rainstorm with dripping fingers.
Wet balls of rain tumble down men's ominous eyes.
You have real lashes, I'm fake as mascara.
My rocky heart boards a flight across the Pacific.
Mesopotamian soothsayers predict a smooth lift off.
White jet crashes on a black runway, a bumpy landing.
Bandage my mouth shut, my mistake,
don't say it, strike two.
Lightning bolts, a stormy realization.
The past cannot be rewound.
A grandfather clock ceases ticking,
short hand freezes at a quarter after two.
Thunder flashes, knocks down telephone poles.
A dial tone hangs up to a busy signal.
Old moon ages from yellow to white.
Black rain hisses; stray cats soar from window sills.
Give me a ring, no proposal with white daisies, just call me.
I would've stayed for a candlelit dinner at seven.
I dangle from the slant of a black teardrop.

Your sensible voice clashes with
moonbeams, lightning, and electric wires.
You say, "Hello."
I put down my busted umbrella,
ask, "How've you been?"

What-If and Maybe

A pair of scissors cannot cut short
the kilometers between us.
It's no use, the length between us keeps
growing like hair after a recent trim.
I measure our distance with a ruler,
compute inches into miles.
The space that divides us is filled
with phone calls, verbose chitchats,
but it's not enough to deter
the impulse of the heart from
demanding more.

I am brooding over geography,
the number of states, continents, cities
where people stand in our way,
faces stern, arms crossed.
I study the earth on an atlas,
put my hands on the four hemispheres,
memorize the vertical lines of longitude,
draw arrows from where you are
to where I am in the world,
toy with the notion of *what could've been*.

We are two dots on a map,
separated by oceans and if I can stop
staring at us for a rational sec,
then I can learn to accept there
is no future, no direction for me
to inch my way back into your life.
The small gaps, the distance between us,

from water to land, I fill it with cement,
watch in regret as it dries.
There are no more cracks or holes
from your end to my end,
as dreamers lay to rest the options
of *what-if and maybe.*

DIGITAL ROMANCE

Mute—
silence is volume turned off.
On a film screen, a cuckoo bird coos,
a gum tree falls, a madwoman screams.
We can't hear noise when audio is low,
but I can feel poetry on your tongue,
your words, void of sound.
I don't read minds, but if you open your mouth,
I can read lips.

Rewind—
history is an antique timepiece.
Scoot two hours, two years into the past,
too many blurred encounters, slurred exchanges.
I can't recall the minutest details
of how we first met, but I remember
the color and style of your hair in daylight,
sandy brown, unkempt.

Pause—
stillness is a black-and-white photograph.
A second captured by a click, preserved forever.
How juvenile and goofy we were,
giggling like children, posing like Vogue models.
How we've changed, how we've matured
since then.

Fast forward—
motion is a high-speed railroad track.
Time whizzes by when we're standing on

a subway platform watching trains depart.
We can hop on, take a ride downtown
or we can stand by as life passes through,
steel wheels screeching.

Play—
action is a cycle of movements,
move into the unknown future.
The End—the credits roll,
monotony in a biopic bores us to death.
Be alive again, my dear, dare to live,
dare to dream in technicolor and sound.
Life is in our hands, we take control,
press play.

A Hai Phong-bound train choo-choos
through the Vietnamese countryside.
Exhaust steam rises from the smokestacks,
graying the dusty sky.
I press my face against the window.
On a barley field, herds of cattle trot,
munching on ryegrass and hay.
I lean back in my seat as the train whistles,
chugging past rural landscapes:
russet mountain peaks, deep maroon rivers,
and lofty evergreen trees.
Across the aisle, a little girl sings
nursery rhymes, *rock-a-bye baby,*
and *I'm a little teapot*, while her father
clips rose barrettes in her hair.
Two seats down, an elderly woman
removes her reading glasses,
dabs her eye with a handkerchief.
Someone coughs in the back row.
We're passing through a bridge tunnel.
Patterns of light and geometric shadows
slip on and off our clothes, shoes,
foreheads, mouths.
Some passengers drift asleep,
some gape out the window,
expressions curious, wistful.
Compacted together, we're strangers
on a train, exchanging polite nods,
brief eye contacts.
It is only when we look into each other's
faces and quiet the complexity
of our minds—we hear stories,
hundreds and hundreds of them.

At Home with Confucius

Let me tell you about a man I memorized,
a fellow by the name of Confucius
(not the philosopher, but this lanky fellow)
who once sojourned to me in meditation.

My vague shadow darting, a cool shade for the brown
farmer nursing his rows and rows of butter corn.
Confucius somewhere over a rainbow solicited my name
in several sympathetic echoes closely heard against

the bump-bump hand beats, the banjo thumping
of my stirring heart. Finding me, his gaze fixed on me,
a certain chemistry, a chemical reaction as the Lord
placed flecks of sunbeams in my squinty eyes.

He chewed on wheatgrass, lent an ear, walked,
listened to my comical theories on nature.
Discerning shyness crawling like red ladybugs
on our green veins, I told him my uneasiness

of rosebuds wilting, the woes of tulips drooping,
how I spied this mother earth as a refuge for grief.
I said, "I laugh when I'm happy, I cry when I'm hurt."
I told him how stares can drown me in rivers.

He did not say one word, not one, but appreciated.
He laughed his crooked smile—sunny, raisin-sweet
against my sanity. The sunken gaze of my remote eyes
was familiar to him, as was the earnest sincerity

he saw I was keeping, corked like his bottled soul,
the tenderness I could never declare as mine.
He whispered, "You're beautiful." This awakened me.
I never told him that I felt very at home with him.

Reverie

A sky carved in half by thunder.
An astronomical split.
Blue lightning veins, fluffs of ivory.

Flat on our backs on olive grass,
alone in a meadow, we are 55 miles
away from the lights of the city.

This is unreal like that Tuesday in Venice
on a gondola, soaked to our bones in rain,
we didn't mind.

A celestial eve—stargazing.
The moon is colored white by chalk,
a glow-in-the-dark eclipse.

We paint a glorious night in dreams,
sleep readily like panda cubs
and during this reverie,

grasses loom high as a fence,
barricading us safe next
to tall bamboo shoots, green culms.

Woman vs. Self

Shadows underwater, daylight slithers,
lowers into the unknown, some place
three-dimensional below rivers
where crocodiles crawl and the waters
glaze orange.
Noon drowses, time blinks.
Eyes open, a poof of light here,
the illusion of a lioness over there.
Eyes shut, sensory overload.
A mind trip, I am seeing things,
imagination defunct.

An umbrella of shade, skies and trees
hover, create a haven around us.
Dry leaves rustle on the embankment.
We wake to the jump of seasons,
reptilian legs creep, calendar months leap.
How long have we been napping?
Changes in nature are evident,
a cold drop in temperature,
the stripping of elm trees,
bald head of leaves thinning.
Our hallucinations, sanities on a leash,
we crawl out of the wilderness,
edge into mass city traffic.

On the avenue of transition,
autumn stamps its arrival when
a postman delivers a stack
of envelopes to a halfway house

where people embrace freedom,
begin second chances.
At the cross of the intersection,
this is the first time I don't feel like
a prisoner of my own battles—
the struggle of woman vs. self.
Release the shackles on my ankles.
There is a freedom to my stride
and over by the river, where the waters
glaze orange, you can hear the roar
of an animal, a lioness has broken
out of her cage.

COCOON

Walking through a long slumber,
the street at night is a black coma.
Silver doubts and quarters in your pockets.
Pick a hand, choose—rock-paper-scissors.
Is this a dream, a midlife crisis, or a dead end?
You can make a 180 U-turn, go backwards
but you can also move forward,
snip off the umbilical cord
that ties you to the past.

I open a window so you can hear life.
Sounds of Chinatown tinkle like bells.
The rain takes a bow as the sun
revels in ovation, rupturing gold,
drying the city with opulent sheen.
Mandarin banters at the marketplace,
women and men rendezvousing
over dim sum and rice wine.
Beeping horns and a violin tune,
a songbird's last hum before
the start of an interlude.

Emerging from a cocoon,
you are a baby chick wobbling
out of an eggshell.
You say you want to live again,
but all this talk could just be babble.
Change is a verb, it expects action.
The first step is getting up from bed.
Put on your suede shoes, your fedora,

look out the window at the streets below.
The city is not in shambles,
it is dressed in crimson and gold,
it is gutsy, it is resilient.
It is urging you to step outside again,
finish the walk you started
so many years ago.

Halfway Home

Drive south. Eyes lit and moonburnt.
Tallow trees slope down China landscapes.
Paddy fields, mile after mile, we breathe
in mist and grain.
Darkness pours. Rain sounds like sex.
We light a joint, bag our troubles,
dump them on the roadside.
This is 3 A.M. driving at its loneliest.
Dead eels in oil lakes. Frozen marshes—
not a crane or lily in sight.
Half the world is in a slumber, the other half
is awake. We're drenched, minds stranded
in a thunderstorm.
We wait for dawn, wait for light to crack.
All winter, you plunged
in and out of gray, begged for luminosity,
said you haven't slept in months.
We're halfway home, sun's ascending—
this yellow is for you.
And yes, the future is unclear, my dear.
Spring will burst with the scent of plums,
and this beam rupturing from behind the hills
is our grand spotlight. You asked for hope.
I interpret it as a sign. The world will wake.
You don't see what I see.
Rays illuminating the curve of your lip,
your brow.
Morning's quiet. You can sleep now.

ABOUT THE AUTHOR

Hᴀ Kɪᴇᴛ Cʜᴀᴜ is a Chinese-Vietnamese American writer from Northern California. Her poems have appeared in literary magazines in the U.S., UK, and Asia. She is a recipient of the UCLA Extension Writers' Program Scholarship and has been nominated for Pushcart Prize, Best New Poets, and Best of the Net. Her chapbook, *Woman Come Undone*, was published by Mouthfeel Press in 2014. Ha teaches art and literature in the San Francisco Bay area and helps several youth organizations promote reading and language arts for children.